Statements

Occasional Papers of the Phelps-Stokes Fund

One Nation, One Country

Nelson Mandela

Number 4   May 1990

The Phelps-Stokes Fund was founded in 1911 to administer a bequest from Caroline Phelps Stokes stipulating that the resulting income be used for the creation and improvement of housing in the City of New York for poor families, and for educational programs for Africans, African-Americans, American Indians, and needy white students. At its first official meeting, the Fund's Board of Trustees passed a resolution on "Plan and Scope" stating that the Fund would encourage publication of "investigations and reports" on matters falling within its charter and "thought to be of great significance." Ever since, publications have been central to the Fund's activities.

Among the Fund's earliest publications are pioneering surveys such as **Negro Education in the United States** *(1912);* **Education in Africa** *(1922)* and **Education in East Africa** *(1925),* the first comprehensive treatment of the subject; **The Problem of Indian Administration** *(the "Meriam Report") (1928);* **The Navajo Indian Problem** *(1939); and* **Slums and Housing** *(1936).* Other works from that period include serials such as the **Phelps-Stokes Fellowship Papers** published by the University of Virginia from 1915 to 1936; **Education, Native Welfare, and Race Relations in East and South Africa** *(1934);* **Art and the Color Line** *(1939); and* **The Atlantic Charter and Africa From an American Standpoint** *(1942).*

In subsequent years, Fund publications include such titles as the seminal **Encyclopedia of the Negro** *(1946),* conceived and begun by Dr. W.E.B. DuBois, and the later **American Negro Reference Book** *(1966) and* **The Black American Reference Book** *(1976);* **South Africa Today**, by Alan Paton *(1951);* **Housing Design: A Social Theory** *(1960);* **A History of the New York State Colonization Society** *(1966);* **United States Policy Toward Africa** *(1975); and* more than 100 monographs, articles, and reports on educational issues and race relations in both Africa and the United States.

This volume, fourth in the Occasional Papers series, presents speeches of Nelson Mandela.

83971

Contents

Foreword   vii

Nelson Mandela   xi

Africa - It Is Ours!   1

"One nation, one country."   7

"I am the first accused."   17

The Freedom Charter   47

Foreword

In his "Report on Education . . . and Race Relations in South Africa," February, 1934, the Reverend Anson Phelps Stokes wrote that with regard to the attainment of social justice in South Africa, "Education . . ., the creation of an enlightened public opinion . . ., and the extension of the principle of interracial cooperation are fundamental processes which have to be brought to bear on a long front."

The battle on this front has been going on for far too long. But now, in 1990, it seems that there may be, at long last, possibility for the attainment of social justice in South Africa. As the world watches South Africa struggle with the process of social change, the moral imperative–an end to apartheid–remains as clear today as it was over a half century ago. This latest in the Phelps-Stokes Fund's series of occasional papers attempts to advance that objective at a time that may prove critical in twentieth-century history.

On February 11, 1990, Nelson Mandela, the living symbol of hope and freedom for more than 20 million black South Africans, was released by the South African government from prison. As this issue goes to press, Mandela, South African President F.W. de Klerk, and representatives of the South African government, the African National Congress, the United Democratic Front, and other political organizations are engaged in talks outside of Cape Town, attempting to craft the structure of a new South Africa.

What follows here is for the record, and is offered towards "the creation of enlightened public opinion": Nelson Mandela's statements made immediately upon his release, and the important and historic "Rivonia Trial" document, made in 1964 prior to his incarceration. If this publication helps illuminate the clarity and fortitude of Mandela's vision, its purpose will have been served. We are most grateful to the Rockefeller Brothers Fund for support for the publication of this volume.

Franklin H. Williams
President

I will stand here for humanity. . . .
–Ralph Waldo Emerson

Nelson Mandela

Nelson Rohlilahla Mandela was born the son of Chief Henry Mandela, a Tembu tribal leader, on July 18, 1918, at Qunu in the Eastern Cape's Transkei territory of South Africa. He attended the Methodist Mission School and in 1938 began his studies at University College of Fort Hare. Following his participation in a student strike, he was expelled from Fort Hare two years later and moved to Johannesburg. He completed requirements for his bachelor's degree in 1941 and studied law by correspondence at the University of the Witswatersrand, obtaining his law degree from the University of South Africa in 1942.

Two years later, Mandela joined the African National Congress, which, since its founding in 1912, had been heavily influenced by Mohandas K. Gandhi's philosophy of non-violence. With Oliver Tambo and Walter F. Sisulu, Mandela helped establish the ANC's Youth League in 1944, and engaged in resistance against the ruling Nationalist Party's apartheid policies after 1948. After serving as president of the Youth League in 1951-52, Mandela was elected president of the Transvaal branch of the ANC and deputy national president under Albert Luthuli. In this latter capacity, Mandela led the 1952 Defiance Against Unjust Laws Campaign. Banned in December 1952 by the government, he was kept from all political activity and prohibited from leaving Johannesburg. At this time he and Tambo opened a law partnership in Johannesburg, the first black law practice in South Africa. However, for his leadership of the Defiance Campaign, Mandela received a suspended jail sentence in 1953.

When the government lifted his bans in 1955, Mandela spoke at the Congress of the People, which brought together the ANC and other political organizations and established a multiracial committee to coordinate the movement. In December 1956, Mandela and more than 150 other Congress leaders were arrested and charged under the Suppression of Communism Act with advocating revolution, and put on trial for treason. In 1961, all of the defendants were acquitted because of insufficient evidence. During the trial, Mandela divorced his first wife and in 1958 married Winifred Nomzamo.

Following the massacre at Sharpeville on March 21, 1960 of unarmed demonstrators who had gathered to protest the pass laws, the government declared a state of emergency, instituted a detention law, and banned all unsanctioned political organizations and public meetings. Mandela was arrested and detained for several months without charges or trial. Upon release, he was named honorary secretary of the All-African National Action Council; this body called for mass demonstrations throughout the country. Hunted by the police, Mandela went into hiding. He became head of *Umkonto we Sizwe* (Spear of the Nation), the military wing of the ANC; leading its efforts to sabotage targets of economic value, he ruled out terrorist acts against persons. During this time Mandela traveled throughout Africa seeking support for the ANC: he addressed a pan-African conference in Addis Ababa in 1962 to raise funds, and participated in military training in Algeria. Shortly after he returned to South Africa in August 1962, Mandela was arrested and sentenced to three years in Pretoria prison for inciting a strike and for leaving the country illegally. When in July 1963 police raided the ANC headquarters in the Johannesburg suburb of Rivonia and seized secret documents, Mandela was brought from prison to stand trial with eight other leaders of *Umkonto we Sizwe* on charges of sabotage and conspiracy to overthrow the government. With seven of the other defendants receiving lesser sentences, Mandela was convicted of treason on June 11, 1964, and sentenced to life imprisonment. He was taken immediately to Robben Island prison, seven miles offshore from Cape Town, where he spent the next 18 years.

Mandela and Sisulu were transferred from Robben Island to the maximum security Pollsmoor Prison outside Cape Town in April

1982. Three years later, in January 1985, South African President P.W. Botha offered to give Mandela his freedom if he would renounce violence. Mandela refused, saying that he would not do so until the government dismantled apartheid and guaranteed full political participation for black South Africans. In August, 1988, Mandela was hospitalized with tuberculosis. Recovered four months later, he was transferred to Victor Verster prison farm north of Cape Town. On October 15, 1989, recently elected President F.W. de Klerk freed Walter Sisulu and four colleagues. De Klerk invited Mandela to confer with him at the president's office in Cape Town on December 13, 1989 and on February 2, 1990, legalized the ANC and 60 other political organizations. On February 10th, de Klerk announced that on the following day, Nelson Mandela would be released from prison. On February 11, 1990, as the world watched via television satellite, Nelson Mandela walked out of prison after 27 years and six months to resume the struggle for a free and democratic South Africa.

Ronald Austin Wells

Reuters / Bettman Newsphotos

Africa - It Is Ours!

Nelson Mandela

Cape Town, South Africa   *February 11, 1990*

Amandla! Amandla! i-Africa, mayibuye! [Power! Power! Africa it is ours!]
My friends, comrades and fellow South Africans, I greet you all in the name of peace, democracy and freedom for all. I stand here before you not as a prophet but as a humble servant of you, the people.

Your tireless and heroic sacrifices have made it possible for me to be here today. I therefore place the remaining years of my life in your hands.

On this day of my release, I extend my sincere and warmest gratitude to the millions of my compatriots and those in every corner of the globe who have campaigned tirelessly for my release.

I extend special greetings to the people of Cape Town, the city which has been my home for three decades. Your mass marches and other forms of struggle have served as a constant source of strength to all political prisoners.

I salute the African National Congress. It has fulfilled our every expectation in its role as leader of the great march to freedom.

I salute our president, Comrade Oliver Tambo, for leading the A.N.C. even under the most difficult circumstances.

I salute the rank-and-file members of the A.N.C. You have sacrificed life and limb in the pursuit of the noble cause of our struggle.

I salute combatants of *Umkonto we Sizwe* [Spear of the Nation], like Solomon Malhangu and Ashley Kriel, who have paid the ultimate price for the freedom of all South Africans.

I salute the South African Communist Party for its steady contribution to the struggle for democracy. You have survived 40 years of

1

unrelenting persecution. The memory of great Communists like Moses Kotane, Yusuf Dacoo, Bram Fischer and Moses Madidha will be cherished for generations to come.

I salute General Secretary Joe Slovo, one of our finest patriots. We are heartened by the fact that the alliance between ourselves and the party remains as strong as it always was.

I salute the United Democratic Front, the National Education Crisis Committee, the South African Youth Congress, the Transvaal and Natal Indian Congresses. And COSATU. And the many other formations of the mass democratic movement.

I also salute the Black Sash and the National Union of South African Students. We note with pride that you have acted as the conscience of white South Africans. Even during the darkest days in the history of our struggle, you held the flag of liberty high. The large-scale mass mobilization of the past few years is one of the key factors which led to the opening of the final chapter of our struggle.

I extend my greetings to the working class of our country. Your organized stance is the pride of our movement. You remain the most dependable force in the struggle to end exploitation and oppression.

I pay tribute—I pay tribute to the many religious communities who carried the campaign for justice forward when the organizations of our people were silenced.

I greet the traditional leaders of our country. Many among you continue to walk in the footsteps of great heroes like Hintsa and Sekhukhuni.

I pay tribute to the mothers and wives and sisters of our nation. You are the rock-hard foundation of our struggle. Apartheid has inflicted more pain on you than on anyone else. On this occasion, we thank the world—we thank the world community for their great contribution to the anti-apartheid struggle. Without your support our struggle would not have reached this advanced stage.

The sacrifice of the front-line states will be remembered by South Africans forever.

My salutations will be incomplete without expressing my deep appreciation for the strength given to me during my long and lonely years in prison by my beloved wife and family.

I am convinced that your pain and suffering was far greater than my own.

Before I go any further, I wish to make the point that I intend making only a few preliminary comments at this stage. I will make a more complete statement only after I have had the opportunity to consult with my comrades.

Today the majority of South Africans, black and white, recognize that apartheid has no future. It has to be ended by our own decisive mass actions in order to build peace and security. The mass campaigns of defiance and other actions of our organizations and people can only culminate in the establishment of democracy.

The apartheid destruction on our subcontinent is incalculable. The fabric of family life of millions of my people has been shattered. Millions are homeless and unemployed.

Our economy—our economy lies in ruins and our people are embroiled in political strife. Our resort to the armed struggle in 1960 with the formation of the military wing of the A.N.C., *Umkonto we Sizwe*, was a purely defensive action against the violence of apartheid.

The factors which necessitated the armed struggle still exist today. We have no option but to continue. We express the hope that a climate conducive to a negotiated settlement would be created soon so that there may no longer be the need for the armed struggle.

I am a loyal and disciplined member of the African National Congress. I am, therefore, in full agreement with all of its objectives, strategies and tactics.

The need to unite the people of our country is as important a task now as it always has been. No individual leader is able to take all these enormous tasks on his own. It is our task as leaders to place our views before our organization and to allow the democratic structures to decide on the way forward.

On the question of democratic practice, I feel duty bound to make the point that a leader of the movement is a person who has been democratically elected at a national conference. This is a principle which must be upheld without any exceptions.

Today, I wish to report to you that my talks with the Government have been aimed at normalizing the political situation in the country. We have not as yet begun discussing the basic demands of the struggle.

I wish to stress that I myself had at no time entered into negotiations about the future of our country, except to insist on a meeting between the A.N.C. and the Government.

Mr. de Klerk has gone further than any other Nationalist president in taking real steps to normalize the situation. However, there are further steps as outlined in the Harare Declaration that have to be met before negotiations on the basic demands of our people can begin.

I reiterate our call for *inter alia* the immediate ending of the state of emergency and the freeing of all, and not only some, political prisoners.

Only such a normalized situation which allows for free political activity can allow us to consult our people in order to obtain a mandate. The people need to be consulted on who will negotiate and on the content of such negotiations.

Negotiations cannot take place—negotiations cannot take up a place above the heads or behind the backs of our people. It is our belief that the future of our country can only be determined by a body which is democratically elected on a nonracial basis.

Negotiations on the dismantling of apartheid will have to address the overwhelming demand of our people for a democratic nonracial and unitary South Africa. There must be an end to white monopoly on political power.

And a fundamental restructuring of our political and economic systems to insure that the inequalities of apartheid are addressed and our society thoroughly democratized.

It must be added that Mr. de Klerk himself is a man of integrity who is acutely aware of the dangers of a public figure not honoring his undertakings. But as an organization, we base our policy and strategy on the harsh reality we are faced with, and this reality is that we are still suffering under the policies of the Nationalist Government.

Our struggle has reached a decisive moment. We call on our people to seize this moment so that the process toward democracy is rapid and uninterrupted. We have waited too long for our freedom. We can no longer wait. Now is the time to intensify the struggle on all fronts.

To relax our efforts now would be a mistake which generations to come will not be able to forgive. The sight of freedom looming on the horizon should encourage us to redouble our efforts. It is only through disciplined mass action that our victory can be assured.

We call on our white compatriots to join us in the shaping of a new South Africa. The freedom movement is the political home for you, too. We call on the international community to continue the campaign to isolate the apartheid regime.

To lift sanctions now would be to run the risk of aborting the process toward the complete eradication of apartheid. Our march to freedom is irreversible. We must not allow fear to stand in our way.

Universal suffrage on a common voters roll in a united democratic and nonracial South Africa is the only way to peace and racial harmony.

In conclusion, I wish to go to my own words during my trial in 1964. They are as true today as they were then. I wrote: I have fought against white domination, and I have fought against black domination. I have cherished the idea of a democratic and free society in which all persons live together in harmony and with equal opportunities.

It is an ideal which I hope to live for and to achieve. But if needs be, it is an ideal for which I am prepared to die.

My friends, I have no words of eloquence to offer today except to say that the remaining days of my life are in your hands.

I hope you will disperse with discipline. And not a single one of you should do anything which will make other people to say that we can't control our own people.

"One nation, one country."

Nelson Mandela

Kings Park, Natal   *February 26, 1990*

Friends, comrades, and the people of Natal, I greet you all. I do so in the name of peace, the peace that is so desperately and urgently needed in this region.

In Natal, apartheid is a deadly cancer in our midst, setting house against house, and eating away at the precious ties that bind us together. This strife amongst ourselves wastes our energy and destroys our unity. My message to those of you involved in this battle of brother against brother is this: take your guns, your knives, and your pangas, and throw them into the sea. Close down the death factories. End this war now!

We also come together today to renew the ties that make us one people, and to reaffirm a single united stand against the oppression of apartheid.

The people of Natal have fought a long and hard struggle against oppression. The victory of the army of King Cetshwayo kaMpande at the Battle of Isandlwana in 1879 has been an inspiration for those of us engaged in the struggle for justice and freedom in South Africa. At Isandlwana, disciplined Zulu regiments, armed only with shields and spears, but filled with courage and determination, thrust back the guns and cannons of the British Imperialists.

When the British finally managed to defeat the Zulu kingdom, they divided it up into thirteen new chiefdoms. Later, they annexed the area and gave the land to white farmers. In 1906, in the reign of Dinuzulu ka Cetshwayo, the colonialists introduced the Poll Tax and other regulations designed to force Africans to work for wages on

7

white farms. The Zulu people, led by Chief Bambatha, refused to bow their proud heads and a powerful spirit of resistance developed, which, like the battle of Isandlwana, inspired generations of South Africans.

The ANC pays tribute to these heroic struggles of the Zulu people to combat oppression. And we are very proud that from the ranks of the Zulu people have emerged outstanding cadres of the ANC and national leaders like Dube, Seme, and Lutuli. We remember another son of Natal, the young and talented Communist Party organiser, Johannes Nkosi, who, with three others, was brutally murdered in 1930, when he led a march into Durban to protest the hated pass laws.

Another strand in the struggle against oppression began with the formation, right here in Natal, of the first black political organization in Africa. The Natal Indian Congress, founded in 1894, began a tradition of extra-parliamentary protest that continues into the present. The next decade saw the increasing radicalisation of Indian politics under the leadership of Mahatma Gandhi.

In 1960, when Bhambatha led the black army, our brothers from India led by Mahatma Gandhi fought to stop the oppression by the British. In 1913 we see the Indian workers protesting against the sugar and coal factories.

These steps show the oppressed people of South Africa in the struggle against apartheid. These steps became an important challenge in the reign of the British oppression.

In the passive resistance campaign of 1946, over 2000 Indians went to jail, many for occupying land reserved for whites. The campaign made clear the common nature of Indian and African oppression, and the necessity of united resistance. In 1947, this led to the Xuma-Naicker-Dadoo Pact, and to the joint action of Africans and Indians in the Defiance Campaign of 1952. We remind the people of Natal of this long and proud tradition of co-operation between Africans and Indians against racial discrimination and other forms of injustice and oppression. Our unity is our defence, and the unmaking

8

of our oppressors. We are extremely disturbed by recent acts of violence against our Indian compatriots. The perpetrators of these acts are enemies of the liberation movement.

The other great struggle in Natal has been that of the workers. In 1926, the Durban branch of the ICU powerfully voiced the grievances of migrant workers on the docks, railways and local industries. In the 1970s Durban workers led the country in a movement to organise and fight for workers' rights. In January 1973, 2000 workers at the Coronation Brick and Tile Factory in Durban came out on strike. They were followed by workers all over Durban. Out of these strikes grew a host of new unions, new union federations, and eventually, COSATU, the biggest and most powerful labour organisation in our history. We recognise that battles won in industrial disputes can never be permanently secure without the necessary political changes. Our Defiance Campaign has succeeded in forcing the government to scrap discriminatory laws and has brought us to the point where we are beginning to glimpse the outlines of a new South Africa. The MDM stands as testimony to the powerful alliance of workers and progressive political organisations.

Whites, too, have made a contribution to the struggle in Natal. It began with the lonely voice of Bishop Clenso and his daughters who denounced imperialist injustices against the Zulu people and who campaigned vigorously for the freedom of their leaders. The Natal Liberal Party waged steadfast campaigns against removals, and its work has been continued into the present by people like Peter Brown. Whites also contributed significantly to the resurgence of labour struggles in the 1970s through the Wages Commission and the Trade Unions Advisory and Co-ordinating Council. Our struggle has won the participation of every language and colour, every stripe and hue in this country. These four strands of resistance and organisation have inspired all South Africans, and provide the foundations of our struggle today. We salute your proud and courageous history.

The past is a rich resource on which we can draw in order to make

9

decisions for the future, but it does not dictate our choices. We should look back at the past and select what is good, and leave behind what is bad. The issue of chiefship is one such question. Not only in Natal, but all through the country, there have been chiefs who have been good and honest leaders, who have piloted their people through the dark days of our oppression with skill. These are the chiefs who have looked after the interests of their people, and who enjoy the support of their people. We salute these traditional leaders.

But there have been many bad chiefs who have profited from apartheid and who have increased the burden on their people. We denounce this misuse of office in the strongest terms. There are also chiefs who collaborated with the system, but who have since seen the error of their ways. We commend their change of heart. Chiefly office is not something that history has given to certain individuals to use or abuse as they see fit. Like all forms of leadership, it places specific responsibilities on its holders. As Lutuli, himself a chief, put it, "a chief is primarily a servant of the people. He is the voice of his people."

The Zulu royal house continues today to enjoy the respect of its subjects. It has a glorious history. We are confident that its members will act in ways that will promote the well-being of all South Africans.

The ANC offers a home to all who ascribe to the principles of a free, democratic, non-racial and united South Africa. We are committed to building a single nation in our country. Our new nation will include blacks and whites, Zulus and Afrikaners, and speakers of every other language. The ANC President-General Chief Lutuli said, "I personally believe that here in South Africa, with all of our diversities of colour and race, we will show the world a new pattern of democracy." He said "I think that there is a challenge to us in South Africa, to set a new example for the world." This is the challenge we face today.

To do this we must eliminate all forms of factionalism and regionalism. We praise all organisations which have fought to retain the dignity of our people. Although there are fundamental differences between us, we commend Inkatha for their demand over the years for the unbanning of the ANC and the release of political prisoners, as well as for their stand of refusing to participate in a negotiated settlement without the creation of the necessary climate. This stand of Inkatha has contributed in no small measure to making it difficult for the regime to implement successive schemes designed to perpetuate minority rule.

The 1986 Indaba solution proposed for Natal broke new ground in so far as it addressed the question of the exclusion from political power of the African population of Natal and sought to make regional change pioneer national change. But we are now on the threshold of a very different scenario for national change. We are on the edge of a much greater step forward, for all our people throughout South Africa. There can be no separate solution for Natal under these conditions, nor can it be argued any longer that there is a need. We believe the Inkatha and all the people of Natal would genuinely welcome a unitary, non-racial democratic South Africa, the goals of millions throughout the country. Our call is "one nation, one country."

Yet even now as we stand together on the threshold of a new South Africa, Natal is in flames. Brother is fighting brother in wars of vengeance and retaliation. Every family has lost dear ones in this strife. In the last few years of my imprisonment, my greatest burden, my deepest suffering, was caused by the reports which reached me of the terrible things which were happening to you people here in Natal. I extend my condolences to all of you who have lost your loved ones in this conflict. Let us take a moment now to remember the thousands who have died in Natal.

It is my duty to remind you now, in the middle of your great sufferings, of the responsibility which we bear today. If we do not bring a halt to this conflict, we will be in grave danger of corrupting the proud legacy of our struggle. We endanger the peace process in the whole of the country.

Apartheid is not yet dead. Equality and democracy continue to elude us. We do not have access to political power. We need to intensify our struggle to achieve our goals. But we cannot do this as long as the conflict amongst ourselves continues. Vigilantes, thugs and gangs like the notorious Sinyoras, have taken advantage of the hardships experienced by our people to profit and gain for themselves. We can stop them, and the descent into lawlessness and violence, only by ceasing our feuds.

We recognise that in order to bring war to an end, the two sides must talk. We are pleased to inform you that we are presently preparing for a meeting in the near future, between ourselves and the present Zulu monarch, King Zwelithini Goodwill kaBhekuzulu. It is my earnest wish that the meeting will establish a basis on which we can build a real peace.

Repeating the call made by Comrade Walter Sisulu at the Conference for a Democratic Future, we extend the hand of peace to Inkatha and hope that it might one day be possible for us to share a platform with its leader, Chief Mangosuthu Gatsha Buthelezi. We recognise the right of all organisations which are not racist to participate in political life. We commend the actions of those who have involved themselves actively in the search for peace in Natal. We commend the joint UDF/COSATU team. We also commend Dr. Dhlomo, Dr. Mdlalose, and Messrs. Nkheli, Ndlovu and Zondi from Inkatha, as well as the churches in Natal, and certain business sectors, notably the Pietermaritzburg Chamber of Commerce. Our search for peace is a search for strength.

As a result of our historic struggles, we, in the Mass Democratic Movement and in the ANC, are the premier political force in the country. This pre-eminence confers on us responsibilities over and above the concerns of power politics. We have a duty to look beyond our own ranks and our immediate concerns. We must strive more earnestly to unite all the people of our country and to nurture that unity into a common nationhood. Wherever divisions occur, such as in the strife here in Natal, it is a reflection against us and our greater societal goals. We need to look critically and candidly at aspects of our own practices which may not be acceptable or wise. We need to be rigorous in identifying our own contribution to the escalation of violence where it may occur. We have a greater purpose than the defeat of rival oppressed groups. It is the creation of a healthy and vibrant society.

We condemn, in the strongest possible terms, the use of violence as a way of settling differences amongst our people.

We would like to see in members of all seasoned political organisations the total absence of intolerance towards those who differ from us on questions of strategy and tactics. Those who approach problems with intolerant attitudes are no credit to the struggle; they actively endanger our future.

The youth have been the shock troops of our struggle. We salute them for the ground which they have gained. Only through commitment have these victories been won; only through discipline can they be consolidated and made to last. Our youth must be ready to demonstrate the same perfect discipline as the armies of King Shaka. If they do not, we will lose the ground which we have gained at such great cost.

The parties to the conflict in Natal have disagreed about a great deal. We have reached a stage where none of the parties can be regarded as right or wrong. Each carries a painful legacy of the past few years. But both sides share a common enemy: the enemy is that of inadequate housing, forced removals, lack of resources as basic as that of water, and rising unemployment. The Freedom Charter asserts that there should be houses, security and comfort for all. We demand that the government provides these basic necessities of life.

It is thus vital that we end the conflict in Natal, and end it now. Every one must commit themselves to peace. Women of Natal, in the past and at crucial moments, you have shown greater wisdom than your menfolk. It was you who, in 1929 and again in 1959, identified and struck out at one of the roots of our oppression. You launched powerful campaigns against beer halls. More recently, the women of Chesterville arranged all-night vigils to protect their children. Mothers, sisters and daughters of Natal, it falls to you once again to intervene decisively.

I call on the women of Natal. I charge you with a special responsibility here today. It is you, in your wisdom now, who must begin the work of bringing peace to Natal. Tell your sons, your brothers, and your husbands, that you want peace and security. It is you who must show them the real enemy. Open the cooking pots and ask them why there is so little food inside. When the rains come into your homes, place the hands of your men in the pools on the floor, and ask them why? When your child ails, and you have no money to take it to a doctor, ask them, why? There is only one answer, and that answer is our common deprivation. Go out and·meet the women on the other side. Their story is the same. Then take your men with you. I want to hear from you. From each and every community, I want a report. I want to hear the story of how you made the peace. We place our trust in you.

Viva our mothers.
Viva our sisters.
Viva the women of our land!

I call on the people of Inanda. Join hands. All of you from Clermont, join hands; Hambanathi, Hammarsdale, Chesterville and Mpophomeni, join hands. People of Ashdown, Esikhaweni, Mbali, and Trustfeed, join hands. Those of you who are from Maphumulo's area, you too. Residents of Durban and Pietermaritzburg, it is your turn. Those from strife-torn Umlazi and tragic KwaMashu, join hands also. I know each one of these names from my time in prison. I know each as an explosion of conflict. And those of you whose homes I have not named, you too should join hands. We are many thousands gathered here in this stadium today. Let us now pledge ourselves to peace and to unity. Join hands all of you and raise them up for all to see.

A great deal of energy has been wasted by our people in violent actions across the towns and villages of this province. If we could channel this energy towards the real enemy of the people, apartheid, we could be free within days.

We have already waited for freedom for far too long. We can wait no longer. Join forces, Indians, Coloureds, Africans and freedom-loving Whites, to give apartheid its final blow. In the process, let us develop active democracy. Democratic structures which serve the people must be established in every school, township, village, factory and farm.

Since my release, I have become more convinced than ever that the real makers of history are the ordinary men and women of our country, their participation in every decision about the future is the only guarantee of true democracy and freedom. Undue reliance should not be placed on the goodwill of the government. It is still a white-minority regime concerned to protect white minority rights as far as it can. Nor should our reliance be placed on the abilities of the statesmen amongst us and our political leaders to negotiate an acceptable settlement. It is only the united action of you, the people, that will ensure that freedom is finally achieved. I call, therefore, for an allround intensification of our struggle. *Siyonqoba simunye!*

AMANDLA!
MAYIBUYE iAFRIKA
[United we stand! Come back Africa! Power!]

"I am the first accused."

The Rivonia Trial Statement

Nelson Mandela

Johannesburg   *April 20, 1964*

I hold a Bachelor's Degree in Arts and practiced as an attorney in Johannesburg for a number of years in partnership with Oliver Tambo. I am a convicted prisoner serving five years for leaving the country without a permit and for inciting people to go on strike at the end of May 1961.

At the outset, I want to say that the suggestion made by the State in its opening that the struggle in South Africa is under the influence of foreigners or communists is wholly incorrect. I have done whatever I did, both as an individual and as a leader of my people, because of my experience in South Africa and my own proudly felt African background, and not because of what any outsider might have said.

In my youth in the Transkei I listened to the elders of my tribe telling stories of the old days. Amongst the tales they related to me were those of wars fought by our ancestors in defence of the fatherland. .... I hoped then that life might offer me the opportunity to serve my people and make my own humble contribution to their freedom struggle. This is what has motivated me in all that I have done in relation to the charges made against me in this case.

Having said this, I must deal immediately and at some length with the question of violence. Some of the things so far told to the Court are true and some are untrue. I do not, however, deny that I planned sabotage. I did not plan it in a spirit of recklessness, nor because I have any love of violence. I planned it as a result of a calm and sober assessment of the political situation that had arisen after many years of tyranny, exploitation, and oppression of my people by the Whites.

I admit immediately that I was one of the persons who helped to form *Umkonto we Sizwe*, and that I played a prominent role in its affairs until I was arrested in August 1962.

In the statement which I am about to make I shall correct certain false impressions which have been created by State witnesses. Amongst other things, I will demonstrate that certain of the acts referred to in the evidence were not and could not have been committed by *Umkonto*. I will also deal with the relationship between the African National Congress and *Umkonto*, and with the part which I personally have played in the affairs of both organizations. I shall deal also with the part played by the Communist Party. In order to explain these matters properly I will have to explain what *Umkonto* set out to achieve; what methods it prescribed for the achievement of these objectives, and why these methods were chosen. I will also have to explain how I became involved in the activities of these organizations.

I deny that *Umkonto* was responsible for a number of acts which clearly fell outside the policy of the organization, and which have been charged in the indictment against us. I do not know what justification there was for these acts, but to demonstrate that they could not have been authorized by *Umkonto*, I want to refer briefly to the roots and policy of the organization.

I have already mentioned that I was one of the persons who helped to form *Umkonto*. I, and the others who started the organization, did so for two reasons. Firstly, we believed that as a result of Government policy, violence by the African people had become inevitable, and that unless responsible leadership was given to canalize and control the feelings of our people, there would be outbreaks of terrorism which would produce an intensity of bitterness and hostility between the various races of this country which is not produced even by war. Secondly, we felt that without violence there would be no way open to the African people to succeed in their struggle against the principle of White supremacy. All lawful modes of expressing opposition to this principle had been closed by legislation, and we were placed in a position in which we had either to accept a permanent state of inferiority, or to defy the Government. We chose to defy the law. We first broke the law in a way which avoided any recourse to violence; when this form was legislated against, and then the Government resorted to a show of force to crush opposition to its policies, only then did we decide to answer violence with violence.

But the violence which we chose to adopt was not terrorism. We who formed *Umkonto* were all members of the African National Congress, and had behind us the ANC tradition of non-violence and negotiation as a means of solving political disputes. We believe that South Africa belonged to all the people who lived in it, and not to one group, be it Black or White. We did not want an interracial war, and tried to avoid it to the last minute. If the Court is in doubt about this, it will be seen that the whole history of our organization bears out what I have said, and what I will subsequently say, when I describe the tactics which *Umkonto* decided to adopt. I want, therefore, to say something about the African National Congress.

The African National Congress was formed in 1912 to defend the rights of the African people which had been seriously curtailed by the South Africa Act, and which were then being threatened by the Native Land Act. For thirty-seven years—that is until 1949—it adhered strictly to a constitutional struggle. It put forward demands and resolutions; it sent delegations to the Government in the belief that African grievances could be settled through peaceful discussion and that Africans could advance gradually to full political rights. But White Governments remained unmoved, and the rights of Africans became less instead of becoming greater. In the words of my leader, Chief Lutuli, who became President of the ANC in 1952, and who was later awarded the Nobel Peace Prize:

> Who will deny that thirty years of my life have been spent knocking in vain, patiently, moderately, and modestly at a closed and barred door? What have been the fruits of moderation? The past thirty years have seen the greatest number

19

of laws restricting our rights and progress, until today we have reached a stage where we have almost no rights at all.

Even after 1949, the ANC remained determined to avoid violence. At this time, however, there was a change from the strictly constitutional means of protest which had been employed in the past. The change was embodied in a decision which was taken to protest against apartheid legislation by peaceful, but unlawful, demonstrations against certain laws. Pursuant to this policy the ANC launched the Defiance Campaign, in which I was placed in charge of volunteers. This campaign was based on the principles of passive resistance. More than 8,500 people defied apartheid laws and went to jail. Yet there was not a single instance of violence in the course of this campaign on the part of any defier. I and nineteen colleagues were convicted for the role which we played in organizing the campaign, but our sentences were suspended mainly because the Judge found that discipline and non-violence had been stressed throughout. This was the time when the volunteer section of the ANC was established, and when the word *Amadelakufa* ["those who are willing to lay down their lives"] was first used: this was the time when the volunteers were asked to take a pledge to uphold certain principles. Evidence dealing with volunteers and their pledges has been introduced into this case, but completely out of context. The volunteers were not, and are not, the soldiers of a Black army pledged to fight a civil war against the Whites. They were, and are, the dedicated workers who are prepared to lead campaigns initiated by the ANC to distribute leaflets; to organize strikes; or do whatever the particular campaign required. They are called volunteers because they volunteer to face the penalties of imprisonment and whipping which are now prescribed by the legislature for such acts.

During the Defiance Campaign, the Public Safety Act and the Criminal Law Amendment Act were passed. These Statutes provided harsher penalties for offenses committed by way of protests against laws. Despite this, the protests continued and the ANC adhered to its policy of non-violence. In 1956, 156 leading members of the Congress Alliance, including myself, were arrested on a charge of high treason and charges under the Suppression of Communism Act. The non-violent policy of the ANC was put in issue by the State, but when the Court gave judgement some five years later, it found that the ANC did not have a policy of violence. We were acquitted on all counts, which included a count that the ANC sought to set up a communist state in place of the existing regime. The Government has always sought to label all its opponents as communists. This allegation has been repeated in the present case, but as I will show, the ANC is not, and never has been, a communist organization.

In 1960 there was the shooting at Sharpeville, which resulted in the proclamation of a state of emergency and the declaration of the ANC as an unlawful organization. My colleagues and I, after careful consideration, decided that we would not obey this decree. The African people were not part of the Government and did not make the laws by which they were governed. We believed in the words of the Universal Declaration of Human Rights, that the will of the people shall be the basis of authority of the Government, and for us to accept the banning was equivalent to accepting the silencing of the Africans for all time. The ANC refused to dissolve, but instead went underground. We believed it was our duty to preserve this organization which had been built up with almost fifty years of unremitting toil. I have no doubt that no self-respecting White political organization would disband itself if declared illegal by a government in which it had no say. . . .

In 1960 the Government held a referendum which led to the establishment of the Republic. Africans, who constituted approximately 70 per cent of the population of South Africa, were not entitled to vote, and were not even consulted about the proposed constitutional change. All of us were apprehensive of our future under the proposed White Republic, and a resolution was taken to hold an All-In African Conference to call for a National Convention, and to organize mass demonstrations on the eve of the unwanted Republic, if the Government failed to call the Convention. The conference was attended by Africans of various political persuasions. I was the Secretary of the conference and undertook to be responsible for organizing the national stay-at-home which was subsequently called to coincide with the declaration of the Republic. As all strikes by Africans are illegal, the person organizing such a strike must avoid arrest. I was chosen to be this person, and consequently I had to leave my home and family and my practice and go into hiding to avoid arrest.

The stay-at-home, in accordance with ANC policy, was to be a peaceful demonstration. Careful instructions were given to organizers and members to avoid any recourse to violence. The Government's answer was to introduce new and harsher laws, to mobilize its armed forces, and to send saracens, armed vehicles, and soldiers into the townships in a massive show of force designed to intimidate the people. This was an indication that the Government had decided to rule by force alone, and this decision was a milestone on the road to *Umkonto*.

Some of this may appear irrelevant to this trial. In fact, I believe none of it is irrelevant because it will, I hope, enable the Court to appreciate the attitude eventually adopted by the various persons and bodies concerned in the National Liberation Movement. When I went to jail in 1962, the dominant idea was that loss of life should be avoided. I now know that this was still so in 1963.

I must return to June 1961. What were we, the leaders of our people, to do? Were we to give in to the show of force and the implied threat against future action, or were we to fight it and, if so, how?

We had no doubt that we had to continue the fight. Anything else would have been abject surrender. Our problem was not whether to fight, but was how to continue the fight. We of the ANC had always stood for a non-racial democracy, and we shrank from any action which might drive the races further apart than they already were. But the hard facts were that fifty years of non-violence had brought the African people nothing but more and more repressive legislation, and fewer and fewer rights. It may not be easy for this Court to understand, but it is a fact that for a long time the people had been talking of violence—of the day when they would fight the White man and win back their country—and we, the leaders of the ANC, had nevertheless always prevailed upon them to avoid violence and to pursue peaceful methods. When some of us discussed this in May and June of 1961, it could not be denied that our policy to achieve a non-racial State by non-violence had achieved nothing, and that our followers were beginning to lose confidence in this policy and were developing disturbing ideas of terrorism.

It must not be forgotten that by this time violence had, in fact, become a feature of the South African political scene. There had been violence in 1957 when the women of Zeerust were ordered to carry passes; there was violence in 1958 with the enforcement of cattle culling in Sekhukhuniland; there was violence in 1959 when the people of Cato Manor protested against pass raids; there was violence in 1960 when the Government attempted to impose Bantu Authorities in Pondoland. Thirty-nine Africans died in these disturbances. In 1961 there had been riots in Warmbaths, and all this time the Transkei had been a seething mass of unrest. Each disturbance pointed clearly to the inevitable growth among Africans of the belief that violence was the only way out—it showed that a Government which uses force to maintain its rule teaches the oppressed to use force to oppose it. Already small groups had arisen in the urban areas and were spontaneously making plans for violent forms of political struggle. There now arose a danger that these groups would adopt terrorism against Africans, as well as Whites, if not properly directed. Particularly disturbing was the type of violence engendered in places such as Zeerust, Sekhukhuniland, and Pondoland amongst Africans. It was increasingly taking the form, not of struggle against the Government—though this is what prompted it—but of civil strife amongst themselves, conducted in such a way that it could not hope to achieve anything other than a loss of life and bitterness.

At the beginning of June 1961, after a long and anxious assessment of the South African situation, I, and some colleagues, came to the conclusion that as violence in this country was inevitable, it would be unrealistic and wrong for African leaders to continue preaching peace and non-violence at a time when the Government met our peaceful demands with force.

This conclusion was not easily arrived at. It was only when all else had failed, when all channels of peaceful protest had been barred to us, that the decision was made to embark on violent forms of political struggle, and to form *Umkonto we Sizwe*. We did so not because we desired such a course, but solely because the Government had left us with no other choice. In the Manifesto of *Umkonto* published on 16 December 1961 . . . we said:

> The time comes in the life of any nation when there remain only two choices—submit or fight. That time has now come to South Africa. We shall not submit and we have no choice but to hit back by all means in our power in defence of our people, our future, and our freedom.

This was our feeling in June of 1961 when we decided to press for a change in the policy of the National Liberation Movement. I can only say that I felt morally obliged to do what I did.

We who had taken this decision started to consult leaders of various organizations, including the ANC. I will not say whom we spoke to, or what they said, but I wish to deal with the role of the African National Congress in this phase of the struggle, and with the policy and objectives of *Umkonto we Sizwe*.

As far as the ANC was concerned, it formed a clear view which can be summarized as follows:

> (a) It was a mass political organization with a political function to fulfill. Its members had joined on the express policy of non-violence.

(b) Because of all this, it could not and would not undertake violence. This must be stressed. One cannot turn such a body into the small, closely knit organization required for sabotage. Nor would this be politically correct, because it would result in members ceasing to carry out this essential activity, political propaganda and organization. Nor was it permissible to change the whole nature of the organization.

(c) On the other hand, in view of this situation I have described, the ANC was prepared to depart from its fifty-year-old policy of non-violence to this extent that it would no longer disapprove of properly controlled violence. Hence members who undertook such activity would not be subject to disciplinary action by the ANC.

I say "properly controlled violence" because I made it clear that if I formed the organization I would at all times subject it to the political guidance of the ANC and would not undertake any different form of activity from that contemplated without the consent of the ANC. And I shall now tell the Court how that form of violence came to be determined.

As a result of this decision, *Umkonto* was formed in November 1961. When we took this decision, and subsequently formulated our plans, the ANC heritage of non-violence and racial harmony was very much with us. We felt that the country was drifting towards a civil war in which Blacks and Whites would fight each other. We viewed the situation with alarm. Civil war could mean the destruction of what the ANC stood for; with civil war, racial peace would be more difficult than ever to achieve. We already have examples in South African history of the results of war. It has taken more than fifty years for the scars of the South African War to disappear. How much longer would it take to eradicate the scars of inter-racial civil war, which could not be fought without a great loss of life on both sides?

The avoidance of civil war had dominated our thinking for many years, but when we decided to adopt violence as part of our policy, we realized that we might one day have to face the prospect of such a war. This had to be taken into account in formulating our plans. We required a plan which was flexible and which permitted us to act in accordance with the needs of the times; above all, the plan had to be one which recognized civil war as the last resort, and left the decision on this question to the future. We did not want to be committed to civil war, but we wanted to be ready if it became inevitable.

Four forms of violence were possible. There is sabotage, there is guerrilla warfare, there is terrorism, and there is open revolution. We chose to adopt the first method and to exhaust it before taking any other decision.

In the light of our political background the choice was a logical one. Sabotage did not involve loss of life, and it offered the best hope for future race relations. Bitterness would be kept to a minimum and, if the policy bore fruit, democratic government could become a reality. This is what we felt at the time, and this is what we said in our Manifesto:

> We of *Umkonto we Sizwe* have always sought to achieve liberation without bloodshed and civil clash. We hope, even at this late hour, that our first actions will awaken everyone to a realization of the disastrous situation to which the National policy is leading. We hope that we will bring the Government and its supporters to their senses before it is too late, so that both the Government and its policies can be changed before matters reach the desperate stage of civil war.

The initial plan was based on a careful analysis of the political and economic situation of our country. We believed that South Africa depended to a large extent on foreign capital and foreign trade. We felt that planned destruction of power plants, and interference with

26

rail and telephone communications, would tend to scare away capital from the country, make it more difficult for goods from the industrial areas to reach the seaports on schedule, and would in the long run be a heavy drain on the economic life of the country, thus compelling the voters of the country to reconsider their position.

Attacks on the economic life lines of the country were to be linked with sabotage on Government buildings and other symbols of apartheid. These attacks would serve as a source of inspiration to our people. In addition, they would provide an outlet for those people who were urging the adoption of violent methods and would enable us to give concrete proof to our followers that we had adopted a stronger line and were fighting back against Government violence.

In addition, if mass action were successfully organized, and mass reprisals taken, we felt that sympathy for our cause would be roused in other countries, and that greater pressure would be brought to bear on the South African Government.

This then was the plan. *Umkonto* was to perform sabotage, and strict instructions were given to its members right from the start, that on no account were they to injure or kill people in planning or carrying out operations. . . .

The affairs of the *Umkonto* were controlled and directed by a National High Command, which had powers of co-option and which could, and did, appoint Regional Commands. The High Command was the body which determined tactics and targets and was in charge of training and finance. Under the High Command there were Regional Commands which were responsible for the direction of the local sabotage groups. Within the framework of the policy laid down by the National High Command, the Regional Commands had authority to select the targets to be attacked. They had no authority to go beyond the prescribed framework and thus had no authority to embark upon acts which endangered life, or which did not fit into the overall plan of sabotage. For instance, *Umkonto* members were forbidden ever to go armed into operation. Incidentally, the terms High Command and Regional Command were an importation from the Jewish nation underground organization *Irgun Zvai Leumi,* which operated in Israel between 1944 and 1948.

Umkonto had its first operation on 16 December 1961, when Government buildings in Johannesburg, Port Elizabeth, and Durban were attacked. The selection of targets is proof of the policy to which I have referred. Had we intended to attack life we would have selected targets where people congregated and not empty buildings and power stations. The sabotage which was committed before 16 December 1961 was the work of isolated groups and had no connection whatever with *Umkonto.* In fact, some of these and a number of later acts were claimed by other organizations.

The Manifesto of *Umkonto* was issued on the day that operations commenced. The response to our actions and Manifesto among the White population was characteristically violent. The Government threatened to take strong action, and called upon its supporters to stand firm and to ignore the demands of the Africans. The whites failed to respond by suggesting change; they responded to our call by suggesting the laager.

In contrast, the response of the Africans was one of encouragement. Suddenly there was hope again. Things were happening. People in the townships became eager for political news. A great deal of enthusiasm was generated by the initial success, and people began to speculate on how soon freedom would be obtained.

But we in *Umkonto* weighed up the White response with anxiety. The lines were being drawn. The Whites and Blacks were moving into separate camps, and the prospects of avoiding a civil war were made less. The White newspapers carried reports that sabotage would be punished by death. If this was so how could we continue to keep Africans away from terrorism?

Already scores of Africans had died as a result of racial friction. In 1920 when the famous leader, Masabala, was held in Port Elizabeth jail, twenty-four of a group of Africans who had gathered to demand his release were killed by the police and White civilians. In 1921, more than one hundred Africans died in the Bulhoek affair. In 1924 over two hundred Africans were killed when the Administrator of South-West Africa led a force against a group which had rebelled against the imposition of dog tax. On 1 May 1950, eighteen Africans died as a result of police shootings during the strike. On 21 March 1960, sixty-nine unarmed Africans died at Sharpeville.

How many more Sharpevilles would there be in the history of our country? And how many more Sharpevilles could the country stand without violence and terror becoming the order of the day? And what would happen to our people when that stage was reached? In the long run we felt certain we must succeed, but at what cost to ourselves and the rest of the country? And if this happened, how could Black and White ever live together again in peace and harmony? These were the problems that faced us, and these were our decisions.

Experience convinced us that rebellion would offer the Government limitless opportunities for the indiscriminate slaughter of our people. But it was precisely because the soil of South Africa is already drenched with the blood of innocent Africans that we felt it our duty to make preparation as a long-term undertaking to use force in order to defend ourselves against force. If war were inevitable, we wanted the fight to be conducted on terms most favourable to our people. The fight which held our prospects best for us and the least risk of life to both sides was guerrilla warfare. We decided, therefore, in our preparation for the future, to make provision for the possibility of guerrilla warfare.

All Whites undergo compulsory military training, but no such training was given to Africans. It was in our view essential to build up a nucleus of trained men who would be able to provide the leadership which would be required if guerrilla warfare started. We had to prepare for such a situation before it became too late to make proper preparations. It was also necessary to build up a nucleus of men trained in civil administration and other professions, so that Africans would be equipped to participate in the government of this country as soon as they were allowed to do so.

At this stage it was decided that I should attend the Conference of the Pan-African Freedom Movement for Central, East and Southern Africa, which was to be held early in 1962 in Addis Ababa, and, because of our need for preparation, it was also decided that, after the conference, I would undertake a tour of the African States with a view to obtaining facilities for the training of soldiers, and that I also solicit scholarships for the higher education of matriculated Africans. Training in both fields would be necessary, even if changes came about by peaceful means. Administrators would be necessary who would be willing and able to administer a non-racial State and so would men be necessary to control the army and police force of such a State.

It was on this note that I left South Africa to proceed to Addis Ababa as a delegate of the ANC. My tour was a success. Wherever I went I met sympathy for our cause and promises of help. All Africa was united against the stand of White South Africa, and even in London I was received with great sympathy by political leaders, such as Mr. Gaitskell and Mr. Grimond. In Africa I was promised support by such men as Julius Nyerere, now President of Tanganyika; Mr. Kawawa, then Prime Minister of Tanganyika; Emperor Haile Selassie of Ethiopia; General Abboud, President of the Sudan; Habib Bour-guiba, President of Tunisia; Ben Bella, now President of Algeria; Modibo Keita, President of Guinea; President Tubman of Liberia; and Milton Obote, Prime Minister of Uganda. . . .

I started to make a study of the art of war and revolution and, whilst abroad, underwent a course in military training. If there was to be guerrilla warfare, I wanted to be able to stand and fight with my people and to share the hazards of war with them. . . . I approached this question as every African Nationalist should do. I was completely objective. The Court will see that I attempted to examine all types of authority on the subject—from the East and from the West, going back to the classic work of Clausewitz, and covering such a variety as Mao Tse Tung and Che Guevara on the one hand, and the writings on the Anglo-Boer War on the other. Of course, these notes are merely summaries of the books I read and do not contain my personal views.

I also made arrangements for our recruits to undergo military training. But here it was impossible to organize any scheme without the cooperation of the ANC offices in Africa. I consequently obtained the permission of the ANC in South Africa to do this. To this extent there was a departure from the original decision of the ANC, but it applied outside South Africa only. The first batch of recruits actually arrived in Tanganyika when I was passing through that country on my way back to South Africa.

I returned to South Africa and reported to my colleagues on the results of my trip. On my return I found that there had been little alteration in the political scene save that the threat of a death penalty for sabotage had now become a fact. The attitude of my colleagues in *Umkonto* was much the same as it had been before I left. They were feeling their way cautiously and felt that it would be a long time before the possibilities of sabotage were exhausted. In fact, the view was expressed by some that the training of recruits was premature. . . . After a full discussion, however, it was decided to go ahead with the plans for military training because of the fact that it would take many years to build up a sufficient nucleus of trained soldiers to start a guerrilla campaign, and whatever happened the training would be of value. . . .

I wish to turn now to certain general allegations made in this case by the State. But before doing so, I wish to revert to certain occurrences said by witnesses to have happened in Port Elizabeth and East London. I am referring to the bombing of private houses of pro-Government persons during September, October, and November 1962. I do not know what justification there was for these acts, nor what provocation had been given. But if what I have said already is accepted, then it is clear that these acts had nothing to do with the carrying out of the policy of *Umkonto*.

One of the chief allegations in the indictment is that the ANC was a party to a general conspiracy to commit sabotage. I have already explained why this is incorrect but how, externally, there was a departure from the original principle laid down by the ANC. There has, of course, been overlapping of functions internally as well, because there is a difference between a resolution adopted in the atmosphere of a committee room and the concrete difficulties that arise in the field of practical activity. At a later stage the position was further affected by bannings and house arrests, and by persons leaving the country to take up political work abroad. This led to individuals having to do work in different capacities. But though this may have blurred the distinction between *Umkonto* and the ANC, it by no means abolished that distinction. Great care was taken to keep the activities of the two organizations in South Africa distinct. The ANC remained a mass political body of Africans only carrying on the type of political work they had conducted prior to 1961. *Umkonto* remained a small organization recruiting its members from different races and organizations and trying to achieve its own particular object. The fact that members of *Umkonto* were recruited from the ANC, and the fact that persons served both organizations, did not, in our view, change the nature of the ANC or give it a policy of violence. This overlapping of officers, however, was more the exception than the rule. . . .

Another of the allegations in the indictment is that Rivonia was the headquarters of *Umkonto*. This is not true of the time when I was there. I was told, of course, and knew that certain of the activities of the Communist Party were carried on there. But this is no reason (as I shall presently explain) why I should not use the place.

I came there in the following manner:

(a) As already indicated, early in April 1961 I went underground to organize the May general strike. My work entailed travelling throughout the country, living now in African townships, then in country villages and again in cities.

During the second half of the year I started visiting the Parktown home of Arthur Goldreich, where I used to meet my family privately. Although I had no direct political association with him, I had known Arthur Goldreich socially since 1958.

(b) In October, Arthur Goldreich informed me that he was moving out of town and offered me a hiding place there. A few days thereafter, he arranged for Michael Harmel to take me to Rivonia. I naturally found Rivonia an ideal place for the man who lived the life of an outlaw. Up to that time I had been compelled to live indoors during the day-time and could only venture out under cover of darkness. But at Liliesleaf I could live differently and work far more efficiently.

(c) For obvious reasons, I had to disguise myself and I assumed the fictitious name of David. In December, Arthur Goldreich and his family moved in. I stayed there until I went abroad on 11 January 1962. As already indicated, I returned in July 1962 and was arrested in Natal on 5 August.

(d) Up to the time of my arrest, Liliesleaf farm was the headquarters of neither the African National Congress nor *Umkonto*. With the exception of myself, none of the officials or members of these bodies lived there, no meetings of the governing bodies were ever held there, and no activities connected with them were either organized or directed from there. On numerous occasions during my stay at Liliesleaf farm I met both the Executive Committee of the ANC, as well as the NHC, but such meetings were held elsewhere and not on the farm.

(e) Whilst staying at Liliesleaf farm, I frequently visited Arthur Goldreich in the main house and he also paid me visits in my room. We had numerous political discussions covering a variety of subjects. We discussed ideological

33

and practical questions, the Congress Alliance, *Umkonto* and its activities generally, and his experiences as a soldier in the Palmach, the military wing of the Haganah. Haganah was the political authority of the Jewish National Movement in Palestine.

(f) Because of what I had got to know of Goldreich, I recommended on my return to South Africa that he should be recruited to *Umkonto*. I do not know of my personal knowledge whether this was done.

Another of the allegations made by the State is that the aims and objects of the ANC and the Communist Party are the same. I wish to deal with this and with my own political position, because I must assume that the State may try to argue . . . that I tried to introduce Marxism into the ANC. The allegation as to the ANC is false. This is an old allegation which was disproved at the Treason Trial and which has again reared its head. But since the allegation has been made again, I shall deal with it as well as with the relationship between the ANC and the Communist Party and *Umkonto* and that party.

The ideological creed of the ANC is, and always has been, the creed of African Nationalism. It is not the concept of African Nationalism expressed in the cry, "Drive the White man into the sea." The African Nationalism for which the ANC stands is the concept of freedom and fulfillment for the African people in their own land. The most important political document ever adopted by the ANC is the "Freedom Charter." It is by no means a blueprint for a socialist state. It calls for redistribution, but not nationalization, of land; it provides for nationalization of mines, banks, and monopoly industry, because big monopolies are owned by one race only, and without such nationalization racial domination would be perpetuated despite the spread of political power. It would be a hollow gesture to repeal the Gold Law prohibitions against Africans when all gold mines are owned by European companies. In this respect the ANC's policy corresponds with the old policy of the present Nationalist Party

34

which, for many years, had as part of its programme the nationalization of the gold mines which, at that time, were controlled by foreign
capital. Under the Freedom Charter, nationalization would take
place in an economy based on private enterprise. The realization of
the Freedom Charter would open up fresh fields for a prosperous
African population of all classes, including the middle class. The ANC
has never at any period of its history advocated a revolutionary
change in the economic structure of the country, nor has it, to the
best of my recollection, ever condemned capitalist society.

As far as the Communist Party is concerned, and if I understand
its policy correctly, it stands for the establishment of a State based on
the principles of Marxism. Although it is prepared to work for the
Freedom Charter, as a short-term solution to the problems created
by White supremacy, it regards the Freedom Charter as the beginning, and not the end, of its programme.

The ANC, unlike the Communist Party, admitted Africans only as
members. Its chief goal was, and is, for the African people to win
unity and full political rights. The Communist Party's main aim, on
the other hand, was to remove the capitalists and to replace them
with a working-class government. The Communist Party sought to
emphasize class distinctions whilst the ANC seeks to harmonize
them. This is a vital distinction.

It is true that there has often been close cooperation between the
ANC and the Communist Party. But cooperation is merely proof of a
common goal—in this case the removal of White supremacy—and is
not proof of a complete community of interests.

The history of the world is full of similar examples. Perhaps the
most striking illustration is to be found in the cooperation between
Great Britain, the United States of America, and the Soviet Union in
the fight against Hitler. Nobody but Hitler would have dared to sug-
gest that such cooperation turned Churchill or Roosevelt into communists or communist tools, or that Britain and America were
working to bring about a communist world.

Another instance of such cooperation is to be found precisely in

Umkonto. Shortly after *Umkonto* was constituted, I was informed by some of its members that the Communist Party would support *Umkonto*, and this then occurred. At a later stage the support was made openly.

I believe that communists have always played an active role in the fight by colonial countries for their freedom, because the short-term objects of communism would always correspond with the long-term objects of freedom movements. Thus communists have played an important role in the freedom struggles fought in countries such as Malaya, Algeria, and Indonesia, yet none of these States today are communist countries. Similarly in the underground resistance movements which sprung up in Europe during the last World War, communists played an important role. Even General Chiang Kai-Shek, today one of the bitterest enemies of communism, fought together with the communists against the ruling class in the struggle which led to his assumption of power in China in the 1930s.

This pattern of cooperation between communists and noncommunists has been repeated in the National Liberation Movement of South Africa. Prior to the banning of the Communist Party, joint campaigns involving the Communist Party and the Congress movements were accepted practice. African communists could, and did, become members of the ANC, and some served on the National, Provincial, and local committees. . . .

I joined the ANC in 1944, and in my younger days I held the view that the policy of admitting communists to the ANC, and the close cooperation which existed at times on specific issues between the ANC and the Communist Party, would lead to a watering down of the concept of African Nationalism. At that stage I was a member of the African National Congress Youth League, and was one of a group which moved for the expulsion of communists from the ANC. This proposal was heavily defeated. Amongst those who voted against the proposal were some of the most conservative sections of African political opinion. They defended the policy on the ground that from its inception the ANC was formed and built up, not as a political party with one school of political thought, but as a Parliament of the African people, accommodating people of various political convictions, all united by the common goal of national liberation. I was eventually won over to this point of view and I have upheld it ever since.

It is perhaps difficult for White South Africans, with an ingrained prejudice against communism, to understand why experienced African politicians so readily accept communists as their friends. But to us the reason is obvious. Theoretical differences amongst those fighting against oppression is a luxury we cannot afford at this stage. What is more, for many decades communists were the only political group in South Africa who were prepared to treat Africans as human beings and their equals; who were prepared to eat with us; talk with us, live with us, and work with us. They were the only political group which was prepared to work with the Africans for the attainment of political rights and a stake in society. Because of this, there are many Africans who, today, tend to equate freedom with communism. They are supported in this belief by a legislature which brands all exponents of democratic government and African freedom as communists and bans many of them (who are communists) under the Suppression of Communism Act. Although I have never been a member of the Communist Party, I myself have been named under that pernicious Act because of the role I played in the Defiance Campaign. I have also been banned and imprisoned under that Act.

It is not only in internal politics that we count communists as amongst those who support our cause. In the international field, communist countries have always come to our aid. In the United Nations and other Councils of the world the communist bloc has supported the Afro-Asian struggle against colonialism and often seems to be more sympathetic to our plight than some of the Western powers. Although there is a universal condemnation of apartheid, the communist bloc speaks out against it with a louder voice than most of the White world. In these circumstances, it would take a brash young politician, such as I was in 1949, to proclaim that the Communists are our enemies.

I turn now to my own position. I have denied that I am a communist, and I think that in the circumstances I am obliged to state exactly what my political beliefs are.

I have always regarded myself, in the first place, as an African patriot. After all, I was born in Umtata, forty-six years ago. My guardian was my cousin, who was the acting paramount chief of Tembuland, and I am related both to the present paramount chief of Tembuland, Sabata Dalinyebo, and to Kaizer Matanzima, the Chief Minister of the Transkei.

Today I am attracted by the idea of a classless society, an attraction which springs in part from Marxist reading and, in part, from my admiration of the structure and organization of early African societies in this country. The land, then the main means of production, belonged to the tribe. There were no rich or poor and there was no exploitation.

It is true, as I have already stated, that I have been influenced by Marxist thought. But this is also true of many of the leaders of the new independent States. Such widely different persons as Gandhi, Nehru, Nkrumah, and Nasser all acknowledge this fact. We all accept the need for some form of socialism to enable our people to catch up with the advanced countries of this world and to overcome their legacy of extreme poverty. But this does not mean we are Marxists.

Indeed, for my own part, I believe that it is open to debate whether the Communist Party has any specific role to play at this particular stage of our political struggle. The basic task at the present moment is the removal of race discrimination and the attainment of democratic rights on the basis of the Freedom Charter. In so far as that Party furthers this task, I welcome its assistance. I realize that it is one of the means by which people of all races can be drawn into our struggle.

From my reading of Marxist literature and from conversations with Marxists, I have gained the impression that communists regard the parliamentary system of the West as undemocratic and reactionary. But, on the contrary, I am an admirer of such a system.

The Magna Carta, the Petition of Rights, and the Bill of Rights are documents which are held in veneration by democrats throughout the world.

I have great respect for British political institutions, and for the country's system of justice. I regard the British Parliament as the most democratic institution in the world, and the independence and impartiality of its judiciary never fail to arouse my admiration.

The American Congress, that country's doctrine of separation of powers, as well as the independence of its judiciary, arouses in me similar sentiments.

I have been influenced in my thinking by both West and East. All this has led me to feel that in my search for a political formula, I should be absolutely impartial and objective. I should tie myself to no particular system of society other than of socialism. I must leave myself free to borrow the best from the West and from the East.

[As to whether] we received financial support from abroad, . . . I wish to deal with this question.

Our political struggle has always been financed from internal sources—from funds raised by our own people and by our own supporters. Whenever we had a special campaign or an important political case—for example, the Treason Trial—we received financial assistance from sympathetic individuals and organizations in the Western countries. We had never felt it necessary to go beyond these sources.

But when in 1961 the *Umkonto* was formed, and a new phase of struggle introduced, we realized that these events would make a heavy call on our slender resources, and that the scale of our activities would be hampered by the lack of funds. One of my instructions, as I went abroad in January 1962, was to raise funds from the African states.

I must add that, whilst abroad, I had discussions with leaders of political movements in Africa and discovered that almost every single one of them, in areas which had still not attained independence, had received all forms of assistance from the socialist countries, as well as from the West, including that of financial support. I also discovered that some well-known African states, all of them non-communists, and even anti-communists, had received similar assistance.

On my return to the Republic, I made a strong recommendation to the ANC that we should not confine ourselves to Africa and the Western countries, but that we should also send a mission to the socialist countries to raise the funds which we so urgently needed.

I have been told that after I was convicted such a mission was sent, but I am not prepared to name any countries to which it went, nor am I at liberty to disclose the names of the organizations and countries which gave us support or promised to do so.

As I understand the State case, . . . the suggestion is that *Umkonto* was the inspiration of the Communist Party which sought by playing upon imaginary grievances to enroll the African people into an army which ostensibly was to fight for African freedom, but in reality was fighting for a communist state. Nothing could be further from the truth. In fact the suggestion is preposterous. *Umkonto* was formed by Africans to further their struggle for freedom in their own land. Communists and others supported the movement, and we only wish that more sections of the community would join us.

Our fight is against real, and not imaginary, hardships or, to use the language of the State Prosecutor, "so-called hardships." Basically, we fight against two features which are the hallmarks of African life in South Africa and which are entrenched by legislation which we seek to have repealed. These features are poverty and lack of human dignity, and we do not need communists or so-called "agitators" to teach us about these things.

South Africa is the richest country in Africa, and could be one of the richest countries in the world. But it is a land of extremes and remarkable contrasts. The Whites enjoy what may well be the highest standard of living in the world, whilst Africans live in poverty and misery. Forty per cent of the Africans live in hopelessly overcrowded and, in some cases, drought-stricken Reserves, where soil erosion and the overworking of the soil makes it impossible for them to live properly off the land. Thirty per cent are labourers, labour tenants, and squatters on White farms and work and live under conditions similar to those of the serfs of the Middle Ages. The other 30 per cent live in towns where they have developed economic and social habits which bring them closer in many respects to White standards. Yet most Africans, even in this group, are impoverished by low incomes and high cost of living. . . .

Poverty goes hand in hand with malnutrition and disease. The incidence of malnutrition and deficiency deseases is very high amongst Africans. Tuberculosis, pellagra, kwashiorkor, gastroenteritis, and scurvy bring death and destruction of health. The incidence of infant mortality is one of the highest in the world. According to the Medical Officer of Health for Pretoria, tuberculosis kills forty people a day (almost all Africans), and in 1961 there were 58,491 new cases reported. These diseases not only destroy the vital organs of the body, but they result in retarded mental conditions and lack of initiative, and reduce powers of concentration. The secondary results of such conditions affect the whole community and the standard of work performed by African labourers.

The complaint of Africans, however, is not only that they are poor and the Whites are rich, but that the laws which are made by the Whites are designed to preserve this situation. There are two ways to break out of poverty. The first is by formal education, and the second is by the worker acquiring a greater skill at his work and thus higher wages. As far as Africans are concerned, both these avenues of advancement are deliberately curtailed by legislation.

The present Government has always sought to hamper Africans in their search for education. One of their early acts, after coming into power, was to stop subsidies for African school feeding. Many African children who attended schools depended on this supplement to their diet. This was a cruel act.

There is compulsory education for all White children at virtually no cost to their parents, be they rich or poor. Similar facilities are not provided for the African children, though there are some who receive such assistance. African children, however, generally have to pay more for their schooling than Whites. According to figures quoted by the South African Institute of Race Relations in its 1963 journal, approximately 40 per cent of African children in the age group between seven to fourteen do not attend school. For those who do attend school, the standards are vastly different from those afforded to White children. In 1960-61 the per capita Government spending on African students at State-aided schools was estimated at R12.46. In the same years, the per capita spending on White children in the Cape Province (which are the only figures available to me) was R144.57. Although there are no figures available to me, it can be stated, without doubt, that the White children on whom R144.57 per head was being spent all came from wealthier homes than African children on whom R12.46 per head was being spent.

The quality of education is also different. According to the Bantu Educational Journal, only 5,660 African children in the whole of South Africa passed their J.C. in 1962, and in that year only 362 passed matric. This is presumably consistent with the policy of Bantu education about which the present Prime Minister said, during the debate on the Bantu Education Bill in 1953:

> When I have control of Native education I will reform it so that Natives will be taught from childhood to realize that equality with Europeans is not for them. . . . People who believe in equality are not desirable teachers for Natives. When my Department controls Native education it will know for what class of higher education a Native is fitted, and whether he will have a chance in life to use his knowledge.

The other main obstacle to the economic advancement of the African is the industrial colour-bar under which all the better jobs of industry are reserved for Whites only. Moreover, Africans who do obtain employment in the unskilled and semi-skilled occupations which are open to them are not allowed to form trade unions which have recognition under the Industrial Conciliation Act. This means that strikes of African workers are illegal, and that they are denied the right of collective bargaining which is permitted to the better-paid White workers. The discrimination in the policy of successive South African Governments towards African workers is demonstrated by the so-called "civilized labour policy" under which sheltered, unskilled Government jobs are found for those White workers who cannot make the grade in industry, at wages which far exceeded the earnings of the average African employee in industry.

The Government often answers its critics by saying that Africans in South Africa are economically better off than the inhabitants of the other countries in Africa. I do not know whether this statement is true and doubt whether any comparison can be made without having regard to the cost-of-living index in such countries. But even if it is true, as far as the African people are concerned it is irrelevant. Our complaint is not that we are poor by comparison with people in other countries, but that we are poor by comparison with the White people in our own country, and that we are prevented by legislation from altering this imbalance.

The lack of human dignity experienced by Africans is the direct result of the policy of White supremacy. White supremacy implies Black inferiority. Legislation designed to preserve White supremacy entrenches this notion. Menial tasks in South Africa are invariably performed by Africans. When anything has to be carried or cleaned the White man will look around for an African to do it for him, whether the African is employed by him or not. Because of this sort of attitude, Whites tend to regard Africans as a separate breed. They do not look upon them as people with families of their own; they do not realize that they have emotions—that they fall in love like White people do; that they want to be with their wives and children like White people want to be with theirs; that they want to earn enough money to support their families properly, to feed and clothe them and send them to school. And what "house-boy" or "garden-boy" or labourer can ever hope to do this?

Pass laws, which to the Africans are among the most hated bits of legislation in South Africa, render any African liable to police surveillance at any time. I doubt whether there is a single African male in South Africa who has not at some stage had a brush with the police over his pass. Hundreds and thousands of Africans are thrown into jail each year under pass laws. Even worse than this is the fact that pass laws keep husband and wife apart and lead to the breakdown of family life.

Poverty and the breakdown of family life have secondary effects. Children wander about the streets of the townships because they have no schools to go to, or no money to enable them to go to school, or no parents at home to see that they go to school, because both parents (if there be two) have to work to keep the family alive. This leads to a breakdown in moral standards, to an alarming rise in illegitimacy, and to growing violence which erupts, not only politically, but everywhere. Life in the townships is dangerous. There is not a day that goes by without somebody being stabbed or assaulted. And violence is carried out of the townships in the White living areas. People are afraid to walk alone in the streets after dark. Housebreakings and robberies are increasing, despite the fact that the death sentence can now be imposed for such offences. Death sentences cannot cure the festering sore.

Africans want to be paid a living wage. Africans want to perform work which they are capable of doing, and not work which the Government declares them to be capable of. Africans want to be allowed to live where they obtain work, and not be endorsed out of an area because they were not born there. Africans want to be allowed to own land in places where they work, and not to be obliged to live in rented houses which they can never call their own. Africans want to be part of the general population, and not confined to living in their own ghettoes. African men want to have their wives and children to live with them where they work, and not be forced into an unnatural existence in men's hostels. African women want to be with their menfolk and not be left permanently widowed in the Reserves. Africans want to be allowed out after eleven o'clock at night and not to be confined to their rooms like little children. Africans want to be allowed to travel in their own country and to seek work where they want to and not where the Labour Bureau tells them to. Africans want a just share in the whole of South Africa; they want security and a stake in society.

Above all, we want equal political rights, because without them our disabilities will be permanent. I know this sounds revolutionary to the Whites in this country, because the majority of voters will be Africans. This makes the White man fear democracy.

But this fear cannot be allowed to stand in the way of the only solution which will guarantee racial harmony and freedom for all. It is not true that the enfranchisement of all will result in racial domination. Political division, based on colour, is entirely artificial and, when it disappears, so will the domination of one colour group by another. The ANC has spent half a century fighting against racialism. When it triumphs it will not change that policy.

This then is what the ANC is fighting. Their struggle is a truly national one. It is a struggle of the African people, inspired by their own suffering and their own experience. It is a struggle for the right to live.

During my lifetime I have dedicated myself to this struggle of the African people. I have fought against White domination, and I have fought against Black domination. I have cherished the ideal of a democratic and free society in which all persons live together in harmony and with equal opportunities. It is an ideal which I hope to live for and to achieve. But if needs be, it is an ideal for which I am prepared to die.

The Freedom Charter

We, the People of South Africa, declare for all our country and the world to know: that South Africa belongs to all who live in it, black and white, and that no government can justly claim authority unless it is based on the will of all the people; that our people have been robbed of their birthright to land, liberty and peace by a form of government founded on injustice and inequality; that our country will never be prosperous or free until all our people live in brotherhood, enjoying equal rights and opportunities; that only a democratic state, based on the will of all the people, can secure to all their birthright without distinction of colour, race, sex or belief;

And therefore, we, the people of South Africa, black and white together—equals, countrymen and brothers—adopt this Freedom Charter. And we pledge ourselves to strive together, sparing neither strength nor courage, until the democratic changes here set out have been won.

The People Shall Govern!

Every man and woman shall have the right to vote for and to stand as a candidate for all bodies which make laws; All people shall be entitled to take part in the administration of the country; The right of the people shall be the same, regardless of race, colour or sex; All bodies of minority rule, advisory boards, councils and authorities shall be replaced by democratic organs of self-government.

All National Groups Shall Have Equal Rights!

There shall be equal status in the bodies of state, in the courts and in the schools for all national groups and races; All people shall have equal right to use their own languages, and to develop their own folk culture and customs; All national groups shall be protected by law against insults to their race and national pride; The preaching and practice of national, race or colour discrimination and contempt shall be a punishable crime; All apartheid laws and practices shall be set aside.

The People Shall Share in the Country's Wealth!

The national wealth of our country, the heritage of South Africans, shall be restored to the people; The mineral wealth beneath the soil, the banks and monopoly industry shall be transferred to the ownership of the people as a whole;

All other industry and trade shall be controlled to assist the well-being of the people;

All people shall have equal rights to trade where they choose, to manufacture and to enter all trades, crafts and professions.

The Land Shall Be Shared Among Those Who Work it!

Restrictions of land ownership on a racial basis shall be ended, and all the land redivided amongst those who work it to banish famine and land hunger;

The state shall help the peasants with implements, seed, tractors and dams to save the soil and assist the tillers; Freedom of movement shall be guaranteed to all who work on the land;

All shall have the right to occupy land wherever they choose; People shall not be robbed of their cattle, and forced labour and farm prisons shall be abolished.

All Shall Be Equal Before The Law!

No one shall be imprisoned, deported or restricted without a fair trial;

No one shall be condemned by the order of any Government official;

The courts shall be representative of all the people; Imprisonment shall be only for serious crimes against the people, and shall aim at re-education, not vengeance; The police force and army shall be open to all on an equal basis and shall be the helpers and protectors of the people; All laws which discriminate on grounds of race, colour or belief shall be repealed.

All Shall Enjoy Equal Human Rights!

The law shall guarantee to all their right to speak, to organise, to meet, to publish, to preach, to worship and to educate their children; The privacy of the house from police raids shall be protected by law;

All shall be free to travel without restriction from countryside to town, from province to province, and from South Africa abroad;

Pass Laws, permits and all other laws restricting these freedoms shall be abolished.

There Shall Be Work and Security!

All who work shall be free to form trade unions, to elect their officers and to make wage agreements with their employers; The state shall recognise the right and duty of all who work, and to draw full unemployment benefits; Men and women of all races shall receive equal pay for equal work;

There shall be a forty-hour working week, a national minimum wage, paid annual leave, and sick leave for all workers, and maternity leave on full pay for all working mothers; Miners, domestic workers, farm workers and civil servants shall have the same rights as all others who work; Child labour, compound labour, the tot system and contract labour shall be abolished.

The Doors of Learning and of Culture Shall Be Opened!

The government shall discover, develop and encourage national talent for the enhancement of our cultural life; All the cultural treasures of mankind shall be open to all, by free exchange of books, ideas and contact with other lands; The aim of education shall be to teach the youth to love their people and their culture, to honour human brotherhood, liberty and peace;

Education shall be free, compulsory, universal and equal for all children; Higher education and technical training shall be opened to all by means of state allowances and scholarships awarded on the basis of merit;

Adult illiteracy shall be ended by a mass state education plan;

Teachers shall have all the rights of other citizens; The colour bar in cultural life, in sport and in education shall be abolished.

There Shall Be Houses, Security and Comfort!

All people shall have the right to live where they choose, be decently housed, and to bring up their families in comfort and security;

Unused housing space to be made available to the people; Rent and prices shall be lowered, food plentiful and no-one shall go hungry;

A preventive health scheme shall be run by the state; Free medical care and hospitalisation shall be provided for all, with special care for mothers and young children; Slums shall be demolished, and new suburbs built where all have transport, roads, lighting, playing fields, creches and social centres;

The aged, the orphans, the disabled and the sick shall be cared for by the state;

Rest, leisure and recreation shall be the right of all; Fenced locations and ghettoes shall be abolished, and laws which break up families shall be repealed.

There Shall Be Peace and Friendship!

South Africa shall be a fully independent state, which respects the rights and sovereignty of all nations; South Africa shall strive to maintain world peace and the settlement of all international disputes by negotiation—not war;

Peace and friendship amongst all our people shall be secured by upholding the equal rights, opportunities and status of all; The people of the protectorates—Basutoland, Bechuanaland and Swaziland—shall be free to decide for themselves their own future;

The right of all the peoples of Africa to independence and self-government shall be recognised, and shall be the basis of close cooperation.

Let all who love their people and their country now say, as we say here:

"These Freedoms We Will Fight For, Side By Side, Throughout Our Lives, Until We Have Won Our Liberty"

Phelps-Stokes Institute Publications

Ronald Austin Wells, Executive Editor

Statements: Occasional Papers Series

No. 1.   Archbishop Desmond M. Tutu. *The Nobel Peace Prize Lecture* (November 1986). ISBN 0-940605-01-5.

No. 2.   Athol Fugard. *Writer and Region* (March 1987). ISBN 940605-02-3.

No. 3.   Wole Soyinka. *This Past Must Address Its Present* (March 1988).ISBN 0-940605-03-1.

No. 4.   Nelson Mandela. *One Nation, One Country* (May 1990). ISBN 0-940605-04-X.

Monograph Series

Enid Gort, ed. *Aging in Cross Cultural Perspective: Africa and the Americas* (1988). ISBN 0-940605-51-1.

Haskell G. Ward. *African Development Reconsidered* (1989). ISBN 0-940605-52-X.

Ronald Austin Wells, ed. *In Search of a More Perfect Union: American Indians and the U.S. Constitution* (1990). ISBN 0-940605-53-8.

Typography: Chronicle Type & Design, Washington, D.C.
Printing: Weadon Printing Services, Alexandria, Virginia

ISBN 0-940605-04-X